Angel Power
Angel Love

Billye Jones

ISBN: 0-9667901-0-3

First Edition, November 1998

Printed in the United States of America

*This compilation of stories is dedicated
to my angels and to all angels who, as we know,
are all dedicated to God's love and His Wonderful Will
and gracious purpose for all of us.*

Contents

Prologue

One source, *The Living Bible Encyclopedia*, states as follows:

Angel [Gr. angelos, messenger], a supernatural or heavenly being a little higher in dignity than man. Angels are created beings [Ps. 148:2-5, Col. 1:16]. Scripture does not tell us the time of their creation, but it was certainly before the creation of man [Job 38:7]. They are described as "spirits" [Heb. 1:14]. Although without a bodily organism, they have often revealed themselves in bodily form to man. Jesus said that they do not marry and do not die [Luke 20:34-36]. They therefore constitute a company, not a race developed from one original pair. Scripture describes them as personal beings, not mere personifications of abstract good and evil. Although possessed of superhuman intelligence, they are not omniscient [Matt. 24:36, I Peter 1:12]; and although stronger than men, they are not omnipotent [Ps. 103:20; II Peter 2:11; II Thes. 1:7]. They are not glorified human beings, but are distinct from man [I Cor. 6:3; Heb. 1:14]. There is a vast multitude of them. John said, " I heard the voice of many angels . . . and the number of them was ten thousand times ten thousand, and thousands and thousands" [Rev. 5:11]. They are of various rank and endorsements [Col. 1:16], but only one, Michael, is expressly called an archangel in Scripture [Jude 9]. This great host of angels is highly organized [Rom. 8:38; Eph. 1:21, 3:10; Col. 1:16, 2:15].

Thus, angels are beings of God's creation, but are of a higher level of consciousness, intelligence and strength than that of mankind.

It is a simple matter then to accept the extraordinary conditions under which any human being would experience contact with an angel. The stories which follow were gathered over a period of years from those who believe that they have had such experiences. Some of those interviewed were friends. Some were almost total strangers. These individuals come from many backgrounds, age and ethnic groups, lifestyles, religious beliefs, and economic strata. Their stories at times contain certain points of consistency. Just as often, their experiences are strikingly different. They are a very diverse group, with little in common, except in one matter. They now all share a deep and abiding belief in the daily presence, power and protection of angels.

Acknowledgments

I want to acknowledge the many, many people who helped on the project. I owe Paul and Dee Carnes for their encouragement and helping me liaison with Pat Bradfield – who was a whiz at transcribing tapes.

Even though I promised not to use the name – it is okay for me to tell Marilyn Austin that I will always have a warmth in my heart for a member of her family – not only for help given, but also for putting me in touch with her. She knows I consider her my coach in more ways than writing.

To my family – I can never express how much your faith and encouragement is a gift. I love each of you beyond measure.

I am grateful to Angela McWilliams for her word processing talent and Defae Weaver of Precision Type for her page layout design. I am also grateful to Debi Seiler for her insights and graphic art talents with the cover design and photography.

To all of you who read all or part of the manuscript and offered suggestions — Virginia McBride, Jean Chaplin, Lucy Konradi, Margaret Campbell, Mary Ann Reese, Ann Tully, Trish Wortley, LaNell Boemia, Gail Warren, Karen Maloney, Barbara Harris, Pat Dotson – Thank you. I may have overlooked someone really deserving of my gratitude – as you come to mind, I promise to ask God to bless you real good!

– *Billye Jones*

Billye's Story

AngelSarah

Looking back, I think that I have always been searching for a spiritual answer to the problems in my life. For as long as I can remember, I have been interested in learning more about how God could help me. For me, through this process of wisdom sought, the yearning for a deeper level of faith and understanding has been like a spiritual journey.

In the beginning, it would seem that what I knew most about was doubt. I had been raised in the church. My father took me every Sunday. Church was a big part of my life, as was my father. I found myself at the center of a very warm and loving family. There were aunts, uncles and grandparents, mother, father and my baby sister. We were raised in a small college town that the members of my family were instrumental in building. I felt very secure and very safe in their midst. I considered myself to be truly blessed to be a part of so much joy and affection.

When I was ten years old, this abruptly changed. The father whom I had grown so to love was taken from me. At that time, the surgical operation to sever one or more frontal lobes of the brain was considered an acceptable treatment for those with mental illness. Daddy went into the hospital, to undergo a lobotomy. His intellect, his ability to respond and communicate, his ability to continue to demonstrate his love for me, did not survive the surgery. The father whom I had known was gone. The man who remained, I would not see again for some eighteen years.

Overnight, the caring, loving family which had been the center of my tiny world, had vanished, like the fanciful notions of a childhood dream. In the years to come, I would witness the breakup of what remained of my family. I would essentially become the mother to my little sister. Mother would become the head of the household. The rest of the family would become a distant memory. With an almost cruel suddenness, all the support which we had come to relish was gone, left far behind in another state. My mother, sister and I found ourselves very much alone, as we struggled to make our way in strange, new surroundings. At ten years old, I felt that I had no choice but to become a grown-up. From that point onward, a part of me would wonder if I could really trust in God. I began to doubt His love for me.

Even with all of the changes, I continued to stay close to the church. The buildings, denominations and participants were not always the same. My mother had never been much of a church-goer. I attended services wherever I could find that others around me would be going. In this way, I came to learn about a God who was not so much in any one place, or a part of any one doctrine. The God that I came to understand was everywhere, everything. My faith grew.

With the financial support of my grandparents, I was able to attend college. It was there that I met my husband. From the very start, there was so much about him that I grew to admire. He even came from a big, tightly knit family. I began to feel as though my life was finding the support and direction which for years had been so sadly lacking.

When our son was born, we were elated. Four years later, our daughter was born. I was overjoyed. There was a boy for daddy and a girl for mommy. We had the perfect family. This would be the family that I had thought lost to my dreams. I could see nothing but happiness in our future. It had taken many, many years, but here was the family that I had always desired. Here was the happiness that I had so deeply longed for. I began to feel self-confident. I began to trust in God again.

Once again, my beautiful dreams began to melt away. My husband contracted a potentially fatal disease. Try as I might, I could not fix him. God began to seem as distant as ever. He did not appear to be fixing my husband either. For the second time in my young life, I found myself powerless to do anything but watch my family crumble.

I reacted by becoming angry – at my husband, the situation altogether, at God Himself. I resented being thrust again into such adversity. Had I not already overcome enough in my life? Did I really need another challenge? Wasn't the breakup of my childhood family enough?

Like the peal of rolling thunder, painful emotions and the memories of losing my father came upon me. In the storm which followed, I came to doubt God and His love for me. I began to feel as though I could not trust Him to produce a positive outcome to the troubles of my life. In my anxiety, and over time, I began to neglect myself and my family. Though a perfect housekeeper, I was only going through the motions as a mother and loving wife. The balance in my spiritual bank account steadily dwindled down until it reached an all-time low.

It was from the depths of this seeming hopelessness that I once again turned my eyes towards God. It was the only place that I had ever known to go. I began praying for answers, whatever they might be. The issue of trust kept coming back to me from my prayers. I quit praying for outcomes. I began to focus upon trust. I turned to my church. I began a practice of rising 30 minutes earlier each morning, using the time to read, meditate and to pray. An unexpected pathway was revealed to me. At its end, were men and women who understood the disease of my husband. Better still, they understood the depths of my own spiritual illness. In time, I grew to know these caring, loving people in a way that was more tender than I had ever known. Slowly, the doubts which had nagged me since childhood began to slip away, to be replaced with the lovingly planted seeds of a lasting faith.

At one point, my husband accused me of getting too religious and pious. At length, he told me to quit doing "all that stuff," and to quit hanging around "those other people." I told him that I would pray about it, and that I would let him know. This was another scary time for me. I loved the new direction that my life had taken, but I loved my husband, too. It was frightening to be faced with what could easily be seen as a choice between the two.

The next morning in my quiet time, I softly whispered, "Dear Father, you know that I have been feeling better since I have been having these quiet times with you. But maybe I should quit all of this, and spending the time with my other people. I could cut back on some of my enthusiasm for this way of life. But God, if you want me to make any changes, I am going to trust You to make it plain to me. OK?"

The following week, my in-laws came to town for a visit. They had driven all the way from across the state in their brand new car. One afternoon, my father-in-law insisted that I drive the car to run some errands. I took the car and, as was my habit, I talked to God while driving. I remember asking again whether I should stop my spiritual work. I repeated that I needed a clear answer. I returned home, I left their car in the drive in front of the house.

That night we traveled across town to where our son was pitching in a baseball game. We all rode there with my husband in his car. Midway through the game, the air began to be very muggy and still. Suddenly, the wind whipped up and it literally poured rain. The game was an instant rain-out. The small crowd quickly scrambled through the downpour towards our cars.

It occurred to me that the rain storm was clearly headed for our house. I began to get an uneasy feeling as I watched the sheets of rain blow through. I wondered whether or not I had remembered to roll the windows up on the in-laws' new car. The more that I thought about it, the more convinced I became that I had left them down.

With the traffic of the game letting out, and in the middle of the storm, I quickly realized that we were not going to make it home before the rain squall got there. I began to panic. The fine upholstery, the whole inside of the new car would surely be ruined.

I did the only thing that I knew of to do. I said, "God, you know that I am going to get in big trouble if it rains into my in-laws' new car. If you want me to keep trusting you, please fix this!"

When we pulled up to the garage, I could tell from the soaked pavement, drowned leaves and flowing puddles, that it had rained a gully-washer here, too. I made a beeline through the house, heading straight for the front drive. Knowing that I was doomed, I grabbed a large towel along the way.

As I came out the front door, I saw that yes, just as I had feared, I had left the windows open on the new car. Figuring that I could at least get started cleaning out what water that I could, I ran towards it.

Pulling open the door, the dome light inside the car blinked on. Light flooded over the interior of the car. To what I can only describe as being my utter amazement, there were only a few tiny drops of water on the inside of the door panels of that entire car. With but a quick swipe of the towel, the inside of that new car was completely dry. I could hardly believe it! With a sigh of relief and a quick prayer of thanks, I rolled up the windows and went back into the house, saying nothing to anyone of what had just taken place.

The next morning in my quiet time, it came to me to keep going with what I was doing. The message loud and clear was that I could trust my heavenly Father, and that my spiritual journey should continue.

I was overcome with gratitude. I was enveloped in the feeling of being watched over and cared for.

In the years which followed, my husband and I were blessed with many things. In time, he chose to join me in my spiritual solution. His illness has been in remission ever since.

All has not been as I would have had it, however. In the picture-perfect world of my dreams, I had always thought that our children would one day marry and raise their family here, where we could be nearby. My husband and I would watch our children mature and grow. We would remain a part of their lives, perhaps even to play the role of the ever-attentive grand-parents. In my dream, we would stay a family.

In reality, it was not to be. The children scattered, as though cast upon the wind. They have chosen to sculpt their lives in distant cities and states. The ship of my dreams was dashed against the rocks of bitter disappointment for the third and final time. Nonetheless, today I honestly trust that the God of my understanding knows what is best for me. I believe that he is constantly watching over me. I no longer think that I am alone.

On a Mother's Day weekend when the children were home visiting – we took a lot of pictures. This time all of us together meant a great deal to me. I wanted to have some photographs to remember it by. In order to finish off a roll, I recall taking the last few pictures of just about anything in sight, mostly of scenes around my backyard. One of these was a picture of our red-haired poodle, Jake.

The first time that I went through the processed film, I didn't notice the angel. A few weeks later, when our daughter was visiting, we looked at the Mother's Day pictures. It was then that we saw her. Looking at the picture today, I consider it odd that I didn't notice her the first time through the film. She can hardly be missed. I didn't know what to make of her. I had never had anything happen in such a way before. In all other respects, the photograph is completely unremarkable. Looking at the photograph today, the outline, the form of an angel cast in an orange bath of afternoon sunlight is unmistakable.

When my husband and I flew to Hawaii for a conference the following week, I put the photo in my purse to show some of my friends. The conference was opened by a Kahuna, or spiritual teacher for the Huna religion. He welcomed us with a beautiful prayer spoken in his native Hawaiian language. The prayer was later translated into English so that we would all know what he had said. I remember thinking that this man had such a loving air about him. I remember almost immediately getting the feeling that I should show him the photograph.

7

After the evening program, I had the opportunity to approach him with my picture. He was about eighty-four years old at that time, and appeared to be slightly frail. He had a twinkle in his eyes though. They seemed to have even more twinkle in them as he looked at the photo. Upon seeing it, he looked at me and matter-of-factly said, "Oh, she is one of your Ouma-Kuas." I asked him what that was. He replied that "ouma-kua" was a name which his people gave to a protective spirit-guide. "Yes," he said, "it is a type of angel."

Before he died a few years later, we had further correspondence. I will always be grateful, especially for his assuring me about what I have come to call my "AngelSarah." I cherish his memory and the wisdom which he shared with me in matters of the Spirit.

So there I was with a picture of one of my ouma-kuas . . . an angel in my backyard. What was I to do with it, about it? Was the photograph of the angel to change me, my life? Was there some connection between the loss of family that I was feeling and the appearance of my angel?

In the years since the photograph was taken, I have certainly done a lot of research into the subject of angels. When appropriate, I have attempted to share my story of AngelSarah with others, in hopes that they might have experiences of their own to share. Simply put, I have been amazed at the truth I have been able to uncover. The stories which follow are from those whom I've met along my journey towards the answers and wisdom that I seek. The people whom you are about to meet through their experiences requested to remain anonymous. They want any credit to go to their angels. They all declared their gratitude for God's love which was expressed through these angels – "To God goes the glory."

May you all get to know your own angels better. They love you and want to be there for you. Read on for the different ways angels have shown up to help in the following stories . . .

Kim's Story

Angel of Mercy

I am the oldest of three children. In 1983, my brother, who was sixteen at the time, was in a really horrible automobile accident. He had to be revived several times on the way to the hospital. Once there, he fell into a coma and had to be put on life support. It is one of those tragedies in life when young people are seriously injured. You can pray for recovery, but not much else.

I was a waitress while I was in college. He was there in the hospital of that same, small town. I would go after work to the ICU area where he was hooked up on life support systems. I would stay and try to talk to him. It got to where I was there a lot. I knew just about everybody on that floor. After a few days, the nurses started to talk to me. They began to tell me how severe his injuries were. They said that there was really no point in his living because he could never have a normal life again. It was hard because he had always been the baby of the family. My parents were clinging to every hope that he would somehow awake from his coma.

This had gone on for over a month. He never revived, or came to, or even acted like he would ever come out of it. Something came to me. I don't know what it was, but somehow,

I knew what day he was going to die. I knew that it was going
to be March 3, 1983, which was creepy, 3-3-83. I also knew that
it was going to be around 9 o'clock in the morning. It was
actually the first time that I had ever had a sense of peace about this
whole ordeal. At the age of 22, I had never known anyone to
die in my entire life. I still had my grandparents living at the time.

I got up that morning and I talked to a girlfriend. She
thought that I had lost my mind. I said no, I think that this is
important because God knows that somebody has to be able
to handle it. I went up to ICU where all my family, and all these
people were. This nurse came out and kneeled down beside me.
She said, "Kim?"

I asked, "What?"

She replied, "What do you want me to do when it
happens?"

I said, "Come and get me and my mother."

About 9 o'clock, it was about 9:03, she came and got us.
We went back to his room and we basically watched him have the
last few moments of his life. Later on, when we were making
all the arrangements, I started looking for this nurse. I could
remember her face perfectly, but nobody knew who she was.
I said that she was a black woman and described what she looked
like. They said, "At this time we don't have any black nurses in
ICU on this floor."

I described her to several other people and nobody knew
who she was. I remember she knelt down beside me and she
stroked my back and it was really weird. There were probably
50 people in the waiting room and nobody remembered her doing
that to me. It was just one of those events that sort of hit me

after the burial and all the horrible things were over. I just thought, that's really weird. I just wonder if that was an angel.

I didn't tell anybody for a really long time. As the wounds healed, my mother and I were talking about it and she said that something similar had happened to her. She said that she was so overcome with grief before the funeral that she knelt down beside her bed and tried to pray, but that she couldn't. She couldn't even pray. She felt this hand begin to stroke her back. This went on for probably 20 minutes. She just knew that it was an angel. She never turned around. She just kneeled there with her arms on the bed, and this thing, whatever force it was, just comforted her. We have come to think of her as an angel of comfort.

Your Name

My heart is like a fountain
Its waters sparkle in rainbow
showers
Sunlight shines through the faith
of the colors
Hope is imbued among the wet
droplets
Gratitude splashes over the
edges

Deep at the center
Where angels play
As one of God's beloved
Your name plays too

Andy's Story

Bright Angel

I had awakened one night, from a dream. As I lay there for a few seconds, thinking about the dream, I heard this loud noise. It was like somebody beating real hard on the side of the trailer. My first thought was that somebody was trying to break in. When I started to jump up out of bed, the noise stopped. I opened my eyes and looked over towards the door of the trailer. I saw a figure.

It started about a foot and a half from the ceiling. It wasn't touching the walls. The figure was about three or four feet tall. It just hung there, floating several feet off of the ground. I realized that the figure was an angel.

It looked female, from the eyes and eyebrows. There was such a gentleness about her, in her eyes, in the smile. It was in the way that she looked at me. She was wearing the most beautiful white gown. I remember that I could not see her feet, because the gown hung down, covering them. Her face was the most beautiful white. Her cheeks were high and swept back. Her features were perfect, exact. She hung there in a lovely glow. I remember the light. There was light about her.

For almost a minute, we just stared at each other. Then a thought came to me. My mind said, "Well dummy, why don't you reach out and try to touch it?"

I did. I reached out towards the bottom of her gown. I stretched my hand out and touched the light. When I did, the bottom of her gown, the place that I had touched, became like smoke. This continued all the way up to the top of her head. Little by little, she turned to smoke. As I watched, she just disappeared.

I sat there, thinking about what had just happened. At first, I was not scared. But then, I started having feelings, scared feelings. I wondered, "Is this the night that I am supposed to die? Is the angel some kind of a message?" I just had all kinds of thoughts. Mostly, I was scared to go back to sleep. It took several hours before I did. I had to settle down some.

During this time, the scared feelings became mixed in with other emotions. I felt a warmth coming over me. It felt like I was being loved. I could feel the warmth of her loving me. Whether there was any message there, I didn't know. It just felt warm and good. I felt loved. I felt accepted, like a child of God.

It took me about a week before I could mention this to anybody. First I told just one close friend. That went all right, so I got to be more brave about it. I told another. It was when I was talking to her about it that I got this feeling inside of me. It was just like that warmth that I had been receiving from the angel the night she appeared. As I talked to my friend, I just got this feeling inside that angels want to be loved too. The message came to me that they want to be appreciated for what they do.

This was what I was thinking standing there with my friend. I had not mentioned this part to her, or to anybody. It had only just then occurred to me. This was the thought that was going through my head, that angels want to be loved and appreciated for what they do. Right at the exact instant that I was thinking this, my friend came out and said it. Like out of nowhere, she just looked up and said the very same thing that I was thinking in my mind.

My two friends suggested that I get some books about angels, to see if I could find a picture of the one that visited me. One lady thought that she knew where she could find one. The whole time that this was going on, somehow I just knew that the angel I saw was not from any book. I just kept thinking this in my mind, "It is not going to be in a book." Several days went by, but it turned out that she could not find anything. I just kept thinking to myself that I knew that I had seen the angel before somewhere. Deep down, I knew that I had.

A few days later, I was entering the downstairs chapel at my church. I wasn't thinking about anything in particular, just walking along. I cannot really explain how it happened but when I entered the chapel, I walked right straight to a poster of the angel which had visited me.

The poster had been hanging there in the church for a long time. I guess I remembered having seen it up on the wall before. I had noticed it. I just had never paid any attention to it. Up until then, I had never looked at it enough to even see that it was a picture of an angel. As I stood there, I looked more closely at the poster. There was writing at the bottom, below the picture. It said that this was a picture of a guardian angel. The second that I saw the poster, I knew that this was the angel who had appeared before me. There was no mistaking it.

Her features were exactly the same. She had the same lovely glow. I remembered that about the angel. There was light about her. It will be easy to remember to send her love.

Elisabeth's Story

A Chapel Angel

Several years ago, a group of like-minded people were building a chapel. About midway through the construction, I joined with a gathering of other people to perform a blessing of the new building. I was asked to pick the place where we were going to stand. I chose a spot by the chapel's fountain. I was also asked to lead the blessing. As we all stood, heads bowed, I began to speak about what I was feeling, and of my hopes for the new chapel. I more or less just tuned in and spoke what I was feeling inside.

I don't remember what I said really, but when it was over, one of the other people approached me. This was a man who had been able to see angels all his life. He said that when I was standing there doing the blessing, that a tall angel had appeared behind me. He said that as the tall angel came, a whole band of angels came and surrounded the grounds of the building. He told me that the tall angel had come specifically to assist me in my work there. Her message to me was that I should not worry any further about any of it.

Much later, after the building was completed and had been dedicated, another indicated that she, too, could see an angel in the chapel. She said that an angel appears behind the fountain whenever anyone approaches it. The fountain squirts twin sprays of water which arch up into the air, then spread apart and fall back into the basin. When the angel appears, she positions herself so that she is in the center of the fountain. The water cascading down to either side of her completes the image of her wings. Whenever someone approaches the fountain, the angel's face lights up as if she is giving the person a blessing. This woman has been to the chapel four times and each time she says that the angel of light is always there.

Some time after all of this, an artist was visiting our church. He is very famous for his paintings of angels. He came to speak at the chapel. This was after the death of my husband. As I spoke to the artist afterwards, I noted that he was about the same size as my husband. I told him that there might be some of my husband's clothes which would fit him. Sure enough, when he tried them on, they fit perfectly.

He said, "I've just got to do something for you!"

I told him that there was no need, that I enjoyed giving the clothes to him. He insisted. He said that in repayment, he would go to the chapel and meditate. If a vision of an angel came to him, he would do a painting of it for me.

When he had completed his work, he presented me with a painting which he said was of "the angel which overshadows the chapel." That painting is now framed and hangs in my entry hall. It was so lovely that I have since had Christmas cards, and even posters made of it.

It should be noted that the last two accounts were received from separate individuals. At the time of these interviews they knew nothing about each other's story. I found it interesting that the same angel from the chapel would also venture out to comfort one of the parishioners.

After receiving and transcribing both of these interviews, I was struck by the terms with which the individual from the trailer had described the angel who had come to him. At the last part of the interview, he was struggling to describe for me what the angel had looked like. In trying to put his feelings into words, the last phrase he used to describe the angel was, "There was light about her. There was light." I have recently become aware that "light" can be an acronym for "Living In God's Holy Thoughts."

As I first started gathering the interviews of others, I began to notice certain common elements. I noted that angels are often encountered against a setting of death or physical danger. As with "Angel of Mercy," the encounters come in some way as a part of a death or near-death experience. It occurred to me then that the notion of a guardian angel may be more than just that. I can only believe that the commonality of these experiences, again and again over many generations, has led to the angel being referred to a sort of guardian.

These early interviews indicate also that at times, without knowing it, more than one person has an encounter with the same angel. The separate, but inter-linked experiences of Kim and her mother in "Angel of Mercy", indicate this. In listening to Kim tell her story, I was struck by how close she came to never knowing the full truth of her experience. So easily, she could have given up in her attempts to locate the helpful nurse. Under the

trying circumstances, she could have neglected to even think again
of the conversation with the nurse. For a long time, she
had no intention of sharing her story with anyone. Had she not
tried to locate the helpful nurse, had she not ultimately decided
to share her experience with her mother, Kim would never
have known the truth. She never would have seen the extent
to which she and her family were being cared for and loved.

There is another powerful message for me in Kim's story. If
there is anything to be learned from the experience which
she relates, it is that there is at least the potential for good
in every situation which we encounter in life. I believe this is
so even with those experiences which are very painful, such as
those which involve the death of someone we love. Kim's story
teaches me that even in the dark times, even in the days when
we feel most lost, we are not alone. We are continually being
cared for. It would seem that a secret is to learn to look for the
good in every situation. Kim's story is very beautiful to me
because it demonstrates that a part of God's love and God's grace
is to help us through things which are seemingly unbearable.

What became apparent to me from early on was that
most people who have had encounters with an angel have quite
often resolved never to share their experience with anyone. In
gathering these interviews, and in my own journey, I continually
marveled at how close we all have come to dismissing these
instances entirely, without ever sharing them with another. I am
also somewhat humbled by the way that my own experience
was so different. My reaction was to seek out more truth about
the secrets of God and His angels. Instead of growing silent,
I was driven to seek out the experiences of others.

How this all relates to my own experience and encounter
with AngelSarah, is yet, somewhat of a puzzle. I just know
that a part of my journey has been to seek out these people and

to hear their stories. I wonder how many other stories of encounters with angels there are out in the world, trapped inside the minds of those who have also chosen to die with their secrets? I wonder if at some point in this journey I will come to understand the circumstances and lessons of my own experience in the same way that I have come to understand the experiences of others. My delightful task of looking for answers and enlightenment on the subject of angels continues . . .

Sharon's Story

Through the Rainbow

W hen my son was about 30 months old, he was stricken with bacterial meningitis. We took him to a children's hospital. By midnight, the doctors told the family that while they were going to do everything that they could to keep the baby alive, they were not sure that he was going to make it. I tried to get in touch with friends, someone to come stay with me at the hospital. I could not make contact with anyone at the time. My son had been put into an isolation unit. I could only go in once every thirty minutes to look at him. Because he was in isolation, I was not allowed to touch him. I decided to go down and wait in the hospital chapel while the doctors did what they could for my son.

I remember in the chapel, I prayed the silliest prayers. I asked the Holy Spirit to have the doctors tell me that this had all been a mistake. I prayed that they would come and tell me that my son just had a cold and that I could take him home. I tried to talk to the Holy Spirit, but I didn't know what to ask for. They were all just selfish prayers.

I tried again and finally got in touch with my best friend. I told her that B.J. had slipped into a coma, and that the doctors did not think that he would make it through the night. She came straight to the hospital and stayed with me for several hours.

After she left, I went back to the chapel. This time, as I prayed, it came to me that I had been praying for the wrong things. In a way that I describe as the light of the Holy Spirit coming to me, I began to have these thoughts. The thoughts said to me, "Sharon, you are asking for the wrong things. That is not really your baby. It is God's baby." I remember thinking at that point that this must mean that my son was going to die. He was in isolation. I could not get to him. I did not want him to die alone.

I remember thinking, "Oh, Holy Spirit, if I cannot hold my baby again, then would you send an angel. At least let her go in there and hold him for me."

After the prayer, I went immediately upstairs to his room. I asked if I could go in and see my son. I was given permission; and as I entered the room, the first thing I saw was this beautiful angel sitting at the head of his crib. I could see her perfectly. She was beautiful. There was the glow of white light about and within her. As I watched, she began to float around my son. The light spread from her and surrounded him. I could see it and knew what it was. It was the same light that had come to me in the chapel.

At that point, the thought came to me again that I should go out into the waiting room and go to sleep. It was as though this tremendous peace had covered me like a soft blanket. I remember realizing that the angel might be there to take B.J. from me, but I was at peace with it. I took one more look at the angel watching over him, and I walked out of his isolation unit. I remember that I did not know what would happen when I woke up. I went out into the waiting room and sat down and almost instantly fell into a deep, peaceful sleep.

A nurse came to wake me up at about six the next morning. I was ready to hear whatever they were going to tell me, even if it was the worst possible news. The nurse said that they did not know what had happened, that they could not explain it. She said, "A miracle has happened. Your baby's life, his vital signs are back to normal. He has come back to us — he is out of his coma."

The nurse went on to say that B.J. was doing so well that the doctors were saying that they might even take him out of intensive care that afternoon and transfer him into a room. When I spoke to the doctors to find out what had happened, they could not explain it. They said his recovery was not as a result of anything which they had done. They said that during the night, he had just "gotten okay." They could not really say how.

There was another time that I believe that the same angel was obviously at work in our behalf.

We were in the process of moving from Baton Rouge, Louisiana to Memphis, Tennessee. We were driving through Jackson, Mississippi. There was a horrible storm. The word on the radio was that there were tornadoes in the area. They said that one had already touched down. They were warning people that if you were in a certain area, you should find shelter immediately. It was very frightening. I was not from around there. I had no idea where we were in relation to the dangerous part of the storm. I didn't know if I was in the vicinity of that tornado or not, but I knew that it was getting so bad that I could not see to drive any more.

I started to look for some place to seek shelter, but all of the safe places were already taken up by truckers or people who knew where they were going once they left the Interstate highway. At that point, I was really terrified. The car was being blown around. It was so strong that we were being thrown all over the road. The only reason we did not have an accident was because basically we were the only car left on the highway.

B.J. was with me. He too was really scared. I remember that he kept asking me, "Are we going to die Mommy? Are we going to die?"

I started praying for the Holy Spirit to help me. I prayed for Her to show me where to go. I kept praying this. I even told B.J. to pray and to ask for a sign. I told him that the Holy Spirit would help us if we both just prayed.

It was right after this that I remember saying, "Oh, B.J. look!"

Straight ahead of us, the storm clouds were gone – just disappeared. It was black all around us with storm clouds, but right in front of us, they had vanished! As we drove into the calm spot, up over the Interstate highway a huge, brilliant rainbow appeared. We drove straight through that rainbow. I absolutely believe that this rainbow was B.J.'s angel helping us. We went on "home."

Linda's Story

The Angel At The Top Of The Stairs

My sister was sick a lot as a child. She had a rheumatic heart. At that time, we lived in a big, two-story house. The scene that I remember was that upstairs, my mother and dad were in the bedroom with my sister. They were putting cold compresses to her head. She had a very high fever. They were scared that she was dying. This would have been maybe 1945 or so. You didn't have a lot of antibiotics and things that you are able to use now.

I was terrified that something was going to happen to my sister, and in my home. I was the oldest child. I felt very responsible for everything that went on in that house, and especially so for my little sister. I wasn't sure that my parents could take care of her. I wished that there was something that I could do that would help her to get better.

I remember that I was sitting on this green, comfortable couch that we had in the room at the bottom of the stairs. I would have been eight or nine years old. I was sitting there on that couch. I was crying. I was praying that my sister would be all right.

I had been going on like this for quite some time. Then all at once, as I prayed, I suddenly felt very peaceful. I looked up, and coming down the stairwell was a very bright, white light. I remember that the prayer stopped, everything stopped. Right there, I curled up on that soft couch and went to sleep.

My parents told me later that I was sleeping so soundly that they had decided not to wake me to take me upstairs. They told me that my sister was fine. They said that while I slept, her fever had broken. It had evidently all happened in a short period of time that her condition had changed for the better.

I knew whatever kind of a being that came into that house that night had solved both problems, my fear and the healing of my sister's illness. For some reason, I also knew that I shouldn't tell anybody about the light or about what had happened. It has always been interesting to me in looking back, to see the way that this kind of information just comes to you. I just had this information when I woke up that it was not safe to share the experience with anyone.

I can still remember the light coming down from the top of the stairs. It was different from any other light I have ever seen. It was so bright. I can still see it in my mind's eye. I remember as it came towards me feeling completely comforted. I have not felt that comforted since.

Inside though, I have always known that it can happen again. I think from that point forward, I have always known that something else was there for me.

Sometimes it seems awfully distant, but once you have had an experience like that, you have had it. Nothing can change it.

Author's Note:

Was that light one of God's angels sent to comfort a frightened little girl? Perhaps this explanation is as good as any other – the friend that told me the experience was sure that was the truth of the situation. Chalk up another vote for an angel of comfort. Thank you, God.

Susan's Story

Her Guardian Angel - Clair

I had a remarkable experience about 15 years ago. It was at a time when I was working very hard. I had a very high profile marketing job. I was on the road a lot, and had been for about two years straight. I really needed a break, so I decided to go back home for a while, and stay with my folks.

By the time that I finally made it home, I was totally exhausted. I basically went to bed and slept for 19 hours. In the middle of the night, I was awakened by a light. I thought it was daylight at first. My first thought was, "Why would Mother have come and opened the drapes while I was sleeping." So I kind of sat up in bed and looked. The drapes were closed, but there was still this light. It was just a bright, bright light. I could hardly see anything else. I thought, "This is really strange."

I looked away from the drapes toward the source of the light. What I saw was a sort of being hovering over this big king size bed I was in. I thought that I had actually died, from exhaustion. "I am dead. I am in heaven." That was my first thought. I remember I reached over and turned on the light. It made no difference at all, so I turned it off again. It didn't make the room any brighter.

I took hold of my arms and pinched them and rubbed them. Mostly, I wanted to make sure that I was still alive. I was so scared that I was dead. That was why I was shaking so. I was definitely alive. I could feel my arms and legs. I pinched my arms again. I wanted to see if I was definitely awake.

I got out of bed and stood up. The whole time, she never went away. She was just hovering above my bed with this long, floating gown. I couldn't really see arms or hands or anything. But I could see her face vividly. She had flowing blonde hair. She had a sweet face.

I sat back on the bed and spoke very clearly. I asked, "Who are you?"

She said, "I am your guardian angel."

I asked, "What is your name?"

"My name is Clair," she replied.

I said, "How do you spell that?"

She spelled out, "C-L-A-I-R."

It sounds funny now, but I know why I asked that. I had known one Clair who was my grandmother's friend. Her name was Clara, but I always called her Aunt Clair. I just loved her, but she had been deceased for several years. That is why I first thought of her. But her name was Clara.

So I asked, "Well Clair, what do you want?"

She said, "I came to say good-bye."

"Wait a minute," I said. "You said that you are my guardian angel. I only now know that you even exist. How come you have to say good-bye?"

She replied, "That's just it. Angels like to have acknowledgment for their deeds, too. We like a pat on the back now and then, just like you. We like for you to know that we are around, that we are helping you. Angels like to feel wanted and approved of, just like you."

I exclaimed, "Oh I'm really sorry. I really do appreciate you. It's just that I didn't know that you were even there until just now."

But then I started to think about it. I am really very skeptical of just about everything. I asked her, "So how do I know that you are really my guardian angel?"

She smiled and said, "Remember the time when you were 15 years old and you were in that awful car wreck? Remember that you were the one that should have died?"

I thought back and it was true. When I was 15, I was in this really terrible wreck. I had been the one who should have been trapped beneath the steering wheel. But somehow, my physical body had switched seats. The other person that I was with ended up being trapped underneath the steering wheel. He's the one who couldn't get out and had died.

She said, "Remember that?"

I nodded and said, "Yes."

She continued, " Remember the year in Houston when you were involved in nine car wrecks? Remember all the times when you were a little girl and got into something mischievous?

She said some more things from when I was a baby. Then she said, "Remember the time, when you were married? Your husband got very violent with his possessiveness and jealousy. Remember how he was holding that dining room chair right over your eyeball? You said, 'Oh God, please help me.' And the chair flew out of his hands, up into the air. He took off because he was scared to death?"

I said, "Yes."

She continued to go through my life like that, telling me about her part in the things I had done. She pointed things out to me. At the end of all of this, she asked me, "How do you think that you escaped all of these things?"

"Well, God, I guess," was all that I could think of to say.

She replied, "Well, yes, God plays a part in everything, but so do the guardian angels. You see, we are assigned to a person for your life. We follow you wherever you go. But it has gotten to where your life is not that easy to follow. Without any acknowledgment from you, I would rather have someone else."

I asked her if she could do that. She replied, "Yes."

I asked her a few more questions. Then I remember that I said, "Let's talk about you leaving again. You see I really do need you."

She replied, "Yes, you need me more than anyone I can think of."

I said, "Please, I will acknowledge you. Can I have another chance?"

I made my amends to her as best I could. I told her how wonderful she was, and how I didn't want to be left alone.

Finally, she looked at me and smiled. She said, "Well, I guess I won't be leaving you then."

It was obvious from what she had said that she knew me, and very well, too. I promised her that I would recognize her, on a daily basis. I said I would remember that she is in my life. I told her that I would show her how grateful I was for it.

Then, we went on to talk about other things. We talked about how I did not feel worthy of having her actually watching over me. We talked about that, my unworthiness. We talked about some character defects that I had . . . my self-will, my lack of confidence, my low self-esteem. They were all the things that I had been working on all of my life. She was very reassuring. She told me that I could let go of those things. She told me that I didn't need to feel guilty about the wreck when I was a teen anymore. She said that I could let go of the guilt. She told me that the person who had died, that it was his time to go.

I remember asking her, "Can I ask you to help me make a decision, like should I chose this or that?." Clair replied, "Oh no, I cannot make decisions for you. I can only help you get through your own decisions."

We talked about all of these things. I finally ran out of questions to ask her. Later on, I thought of a bunch more things.

Right then, that is all that I could think of to talk about. It was such a shock, the dramatic way in which she appeared. I just didn't really know what to do.

I remember telling her that I really couldn't think of anything else to ask her. I asked if there was anything else that she wanted to tell me. She talked more about angels and about their needs. I remember thinking that the kinds of things that they must need were exactly the same kinds of things that I was needing in my own life right then. I remember thinking, "Wow, what a coincidence."

Then, I asked her how long she had been with me. She replied, "I have always been with you."

At that point, I was still so very tired. I had only been asleep for a few hours when this all happened. I did not know what to do at this point. I did not just want to ask her to leave, but I had to go back to sleep.

So I said, "Well, I guess that I will go back to sleep now."

But she did not leave. She was so bright and she was still there.

I did not know what else to do. I asked her, "Would you like to lie down with me?"

She said, "Sure." So I just kind of fluffed up her pillow on the other side of that big, king size bed. She just floated down and put her head on the pillow. I said goodnight. I closed my eyes and I was asleep immediately.

Within a few hours, the phone rang and woke me up. I had more or less forgotten where I was. Once I realized that I was in my folks house, I looked for the phone. There was one on a little stand about six or eight feet away from the bed. I really wasn't quite awake yet. I did not quite remember where I was. I was so used to being in a hotel room that I got up and walked over to answer the phone. When I answered, my mother was already on the line. So when I picked it up, she had just started talking to whomever had called. I could tell by the voice that it was an aunt of mine. She was crying. She said that she was taking her own life. She would not tell my mother where she was.

She said she had made her decision and that life was not worth living anymore. She told Mother that it was just too painful. I remember that I could hear the pain in her voice. I could truly feel it. She said, "You cannot talk me out of it. I love you so much. You have all helped me so much. I wanted to tell you good-bye." Then, she hung up and the line went dead.

I could hear Mother and Daddy stirring upstairs. They were really freaking out. They did not know what to do. I did the only thing I could think of under the circumstances. I asked my angel, "Clair, would you mind going to my aunt? Could you please help her out of this?"

I lay back down and went back to sleep. I slept very peacefully. A few hours later, the phone rang. Just as before, the exact same thing happened. I was still half asleep, but I walked over and picked up the phone. Again, I heard Mother already talking to someone. It wasn't even as if I was eavesdropping. It was as if I was supposed to be listening to what was going on.

It was my aunt again. I heard her say to my mother, "Oh you would not believe what has happened." Her voice was so full of joy that I could hardly believe it. She said, "I have never been happier, more peaceful, more serene." Whatever had happened, it was obvious that now she was fine.

My aunt continued, "Almost instantly, when we hung up the phone before, this peaceful feeling that everything was going to be all right came over me. I felt as though everything was happening in divine order in my life. The feeling came over me so suddenly and was so powerful that I have never wanted to live more than I want to live right now."

As I hung up the phone and walked back towards the bed, a chill and goosebumps washed over me. I looked around to see if Clair had come back. I said, "Are you back?" There was no response, nothing.

I said, "You can come back now. Thank you for the miracle you have done." As I stood there, I began to understand what had happened. Because I have always discounted things, without this incident with my aunt, I don't think that, in the morning, I would have really believed this had happened. I would have just written it off as something I had dreamed.

The next morning, when I finally woke up, I was thinking abut the night before. I thought, "Who in the world am I going to tell this to? They all will think I am crazy."

This was at a time when nobody that I knew would go around talking about angels. I certainly did not know anything about them. At that point, I probably would not have believed anybody else's angel story. I believed mine though.

Later, I was sitting in the kitchen with my mother. I was not talking much. I was thinking. I thought, "Now who can I tell?"

One by one, I thought through all of my friends, everyone that I know. I thought, "I do not know a single person whom I can tell this to."

Then, the thought hit me. I could tell it to Mother. It occurred to me that if I told my mother, she would understand. She may or may not believe me, but she wouldn't burst out laughing or anything.

This had been such an incredible experience, I was just busting to tell someone. I just had to tell someone.

So, Mother was asking me if she could fix me anything to eat. I said, "No, I am not really that hungry. But I would like to talk to you."

She said, "Well honey, at least eat first."

She was really into her Mom thing. But I said, "No, I just really have to talk to you."

When she saw the look on my face, she sat down at the table with me and I told her the whole story. She listened all the way through and did not even make a comment. When I was finished, she got up from the table. She said, "You just wait right here. I am going to try and find something."

She was gone for the longest time. After about thirty minutes, I finally went to go find her. She was in her bedroom, on the floor, crawling around in her closet. She rummaged through a lot of old stuff. I said, "What in the world are you doing?"

She said, "Just leave the room. I'll be out in a minute."

She never talks to me like that, so I did what she asked. She finally came out. She was carrying this little pink book in her hands. I asked, "What is that Mother?"

She told me about a woman whom she had met some ten years earlier. The woman had known her and had known me. At least, she knew that I was Mother's daughter. That was about it. Anyway, this lady had given Mother a little book. She told her to save it for me because one day I would need it. She would not tell Mother anything else. Mother said that she had taken one look at the book and had told the lady, "Well I can guarantee you that she is not going to read anything like this."

Mother said the lady had replied, "No she won't. You don't need to tell her that you have it. Just save it for her. You will know when she needs it." With that as an explanation, Mother handed me this little pink book.

I sat down to look at it and Mother said, "What I want you to do is look through the book. I have no earthly idea what you are going to find, just flip through the book."

So, I flipped through it real fast, thinking that this was ridiculous. I did not find anything, so I handed the book back to her. She said, "No, go slow. I want you to do this page by page."

She had patiently sat and listened to my story. I figured that I might as well do what she was asking me to do. I went back through the book. This time, I went through it carefully, looking at every page. All of a sudden, there was Clair's picture, clear as day. It said at the bottom of the page "Guardian Angel."

Now I am not saying that everyone's guardian angel looks like that. I am just saying that for me, I know that I needed to have that kind of proof. Otherwise, I never could have believed that something so good was happening to me. I never would have believed that it was all real.

I still have that little picture. I still have Clair with me each day. She remains a stabilizing, calming force in my life. She's here. She's always here.

Along The Journey . . .

It is clear that the presence of our angels becomes most apparent during episodes of trauma, or where a person's life is being threatened. In these extreme cases, it is almost as if the angels have no other choice but to resort to extraordinary measures to protect the lives, the physical bodies of God's precious children. Under these circumstances, they seem to have no other choice but to reveal their presence – often through some form of miraculous intervention. The accounts gathered during the first part of my journey clearly indicate this.

Still, as I continued to gather these stories, another level of understanding began to come clear to me. I began to see that many of the stories seem to indicate that the person's angel had been with them for much longer than just during the trying time. The story of Clair is just such an occurrence. As I spoke with more people, and as my own understanding of the power of angels began to grow, I realized that our angels are with us each and every day. As Clair herself indicated, the secret to tapping into the power of one's angel is to first recognize their presence. Perhaps it is just the natural order of things that we are at first very skeptical of such extraordinary things.

In time, I began to see, however, that once a person acknowledges the presence of their angelic companions, once they learn to accept their guidance, once they begin to return their love, a peace and serenity begins to wash over them. As in the story of *The Angel At The Top Of The Stairs*, the end result of that powerful experience was not so much that the person was healed and made well. What really occurred, was that this person was left with the feeling of knowing, really knowing that she was never alone in this world. She knew that her angel would always be there to help her. From that point on, she would always feel from deep within her a level of understanding and faith that nothing could take away. A feeling of spiritual completeness, of being truly comforted, would be with her always.

I believe that it must be like this for all of us who have opened our hearts to the presence of God and His loving angels. There, in the stillness of our hearts, we will always know that His love for us is a constant and living thing. Once we have experienced some level of contact with our angels, deep down inside, our spirit will forever after be at peace.

Charlotte's Angel

When I was about eleven years old, my mother and my father had gone through a divorce. She was going through this period of trying to find herself. She ended up dating a married man. They had broken up. Although I did not know it at the time, she decided to commit suicide.

At that time, Mother was going to night school, trying to further her education. She was trying to do something which would help her to find a better job. This was one of those school nights when she was usually going to be gone. Mother had told me earlier in the day that she was going to be gone that night. She said that she would be taking me down to the babysitter's house.

That night, before we left, Mother was ironing. I was sitting there watching her, waiting for us to leave. As I watched, this glow came up over the end of the ironing board. It was made up of pretty colors, blue and white and pastels. There were colors so beautiful that I cannot even tell you what they looked like.

Then, I saw a face appear out of the glow. Next, I saw a wing. Only it wasn't a wing like you would think of one being. The wing that I saw was more like a flowing curvature of dancing light. The face was soft and glowing. I can't even give you any definite description of it. What I saw just looked like an angel, and it was rising up at the end of my mother's ironing board.

I saw her, but apparently my mother didn't. I asked, "Momma, do you see something there, at the foot of the ironing board?"

She replied, "No I don't Charlotte. I just don't."

I said to her, "But Momma, there is something there. It looks like an angel."

Mother said, "I don't see her. . . you go on and play now. I'll take you down to the babysitter's as soon as I am finished."

She took me down to the babysitter's. It was about a block away from our house. I am not sure what time it was; it was dark outside, night time. I had no hint to make me believe that my mother was planning anything out of the ordinary. As with any other of her school nights, she just dropped me off at the sitter's and left.

I remember that later, maybe eleven or twelve o'clock it seemed to me, I could not sleep. I was lying there awake. At first, I did not see the angel again. Instead, I felt something pick me up by the shoulders. It was just like it pushed my feet out of the bed, put them on the floor and stood me up. Then, I felt something like an arm being around me. It was walking me to my home. I didn't know where I was going, what I was doing or what was happening to me.

This thing, that sort of felt like an arm, stayed wrapped around me. It walked me all the way home. When we got closer, the house was pitch black. That was different, because my mother always left a light on. As we came up towards the door, a light came on in the house. I didn't turn it on. We weren't even up to the house yet. Nobody turned it on. The light just came on by itself.

Then I saw the glow again, just in front of me. I realized that I was seeing the backside of the angel. She was leading me to the house. I was totally mesmerized. I could only follow along right behind her.

She lead me through the house. When we got to the bathroom, it was as if something took my hand and flipped on the light switch. I saw my mother, lying on the floor. That was back in the fifties. Houses still had gas space heaters in the bathrooms. My mother had tried to gas herself to death.

I didn't turn the stove off. I don't know who did, unless it was the angel. At the same time that I found my mother, I realized that all at once, the lights had come on in the house. I looked around for the angel. She was suddenly nowhere near. Just as suddenly, I felt cold. It was like the strength had gone away from me. That is when I came back also – from being somewhere else – at least another state of consciousness. Everything returned to normal. I remember that I was standing there, watching my mother lay there on the floor. I remember the emotions that washed over me as I stood looking at her. With the angel gone, I felt scared and alone.

I called an ambulance. They came. I don't remember much of what happened after that.

I do remember thinking about the angel. I kept thinking and thinking about her. I couldn't stop thinking about her. I was scared to death to tell anybody what had really happened.

I felt that nobody would believe me, especially me being just
an eleven-year-old kid. So, I just kept it to myself, for many,
many years.

I don't know exactly how many years it was after this
happened that one day I was reading *Reader's Digest*. I happened
upon an article about guardian angels and children and leading the
children and helping others out of danger. I wish I could find it
again. I have continued to look for it. I felt as if the article
validated my experience.

At any rate, ever since then, I have come to think of this as
a guardian angel experience. I do not know if it was my guardian
angel or her's which helped me. The angel was definitely what
I would call a guardian angel. She was so beautiful. I knew that
she was an angel. I know too that I certainly would not have
gotten up on my own and walked back home that night. I had
no way of knowing that anything was wrong. I believe that it was
not my mother's time to go, and that God sent the angel to me,
so I could go help my mother.

You should understand that I did not discuss any of what
happened that night with my mother. In fact, I didn't talk about
the angel to anyone.

There were two other experiences which are a part of all
of this. They happened years later.

My family is of Native American descent. I am Choctaw
Indian. My grandmother lived on a reservation when she
was a child. My mother grew up in Oklahoma, around an Indian
reservation. When my grandmother was dying, my mother had
gone to be with her. Just before my grandmother died, apparently
she looked at my mother and said calmly, "I am fixing to go.
The angels are here." With that, she closed her eyes and died. It
was as if she just peacefully "went to sleep."

This last June, Mother had cancer surgery. After the surgery, I was very worried about her. She told me very matter-of-factly that I shouldn't be. She said, "I am not going to die yet."

I asked her how she could know. It was at that point that she told me about what my grandmother had said as she died. Then Mother said, "I will know that I am to go when they come for me. They will be singing and they will cradle me."

I said, "Who Momma? Who will come for you?"

She replied, "The angels."

I asked her, "But how can you know this?"

She smiled and said, "Because one is here with me right now, child, holding my hand."

This time, I couldn't see the angel. But I asked her, "Momma, what does it look like?"

She said, "Oh Charlotte, I can't describe her to you. She is so beautiful. She is just shimmering light, with more energy than you can imagine. The only portion of her that looks human is the face. There are like eyes, and a nose, the rest is just a blending of light. The only other things that I can see are her wings. They are just a glowing, white light."

Looking into the palm of her own outstretched hand, she finished her description by saying, "And I can see her beautiful, glowing hand. I feel safe with her here. I feel so safe."

Charlotte finished telling her story by saying, "She was describing the angel I had been with that time long ago. I am so grateful to God for the experiences and that my mother lived out her life span."

Delane's Story

An Angel's Touch

When I was a little girl, I had a friend who lived up the hill from what used to be the Edwards Ranch in Fort Worth, Texas. This was just before the ranch land was to be developed. All of the land had been bought for what is now the Tanglewood section of the city. There were big, concrete storm sewer pipes laying all along the top of the ground, waiting to be buried.

My friend invited me to her house to play one afternoon after school. We had the best time running all around the ranch and playing around in those pipes. We were both tomboys. We had a great time.

When it was time to quit, she wanted to go back to her house a different way. We had to cross a rushing stream. I was a good swimmer, but not in that kind of water. I did not want to cross.

She said, "Oh come on. It will be all right. I have done this lots of times."

I told her that I was still not going to cross. She replied, "It's not even deep. We can just wade across."

As if to prove it, she went right on into the water. She waded across to the other side and headed on up the hill on the other side. She made it look so easy that I would have felt silly not following her.

I stepped into the water. I was up to my neck in water almost instantly. The water was rushing all around me. I was afraid that I was going to drown. I tried to turn around, to get back up on the shore. When I tried to move, I realized that my foot was stuck. The shoe had become wedged in the caliche rocks at the bottom of the stream.

The current from the rushing water was pushing me downstream. With my foot stuck, the weight of all the water started to push me under. I became very, very frightened. I tried to reach out and grab for an overhanging branch attached to a tree on the other bank of the stream. As hard as I tried, I could not reach it. The current was starting to pull me under.

The next thing I knew, I was sitting down on the other side. I don't remember getting out of the water. It was as if an invisible force had reached down and lifted me up out of the water and placed me safely on the bank.

I don't know if it was a guardian angel or what. Something just lifted me out of the water, and over to the other bank.

I remember standing there all wet, and with only one shoe. I had lost the other one in the water. I was a mess. [My grandmother – who lived with us – was very particular about my clothes. She starched and pressed them. I looked like a little doll when I went to school]. I was very afraid about going home with wet, wrinkled clothes, and only one shoe. However, miraculously when I got home this time, nobody even noticed my disheveled appearance.

I might have dismissed this first incident as being just luck, a lapse of memory, whatever. Except that I had another profound experience years later...

I was going through a divorce. My son was about eight months old. We were involved in a terrible custody battle. It was really awful. I was afraid my ex-husband would try to take my baby away from me.

I went to my church regularly. I talked to my priest about everything. He assured me that I was doing the right thing. He said if it became necessary he would support me in court.

After our talk, I walked back to my car. I was holding my son in my right arm. I reached for the door handle of the car with my left hand. As I did, I felt three very distinct pats on my shoulder.

They were pats like someone does when they are patting your shoulder to let you know that everything is going to be all right. [It also felt like a masculine presence].

My immediate thought was, "How did the priest get out here so fast? I wonder what he wants to tell me? I thought we had finished our conversation." [You know how quickly those type of thoughts can go through your mind].

I turned around to speak with him, and there was no one there. There was not another visible soul in the parking lot. There was not another car. There weren't the disappearing robes of the priest – there was just seeming empty space.

My first thought was that it was an angel watching over me. Before I turned around, I remembered that I sensed a very masculine powerful presence there with me. At the time, as I was turning to speak, I thought it was the priest.

When there was no one there, I knew that it was an angel. The angel (for that is what I have come to believe that indeed it was an angel) had a message for me . . . " You don't need to worry about all of these things. I'm right here looking out for you."

The situation which I previously was dreading was that my husband would come to the divorce proceedings with false evidence questioning my being a fit mother. I was so afraid that the court would take my baby away. At that point in my life I thought that courts and judges had all the power over things in life. When we finally did go to court, the subject did not even come up. It was dropped entirely. Needless to say, my faith in God's goodness and His angelic help has been a strong belief ever since. Thank you, God. "God is so good. God is so good. God is so good. He's so good to me. God is my help in every need. God is so good."

Nancy's Story

The Gift of The Angels

round 1970, I went through a very traumatic divorce. I was very emotionally unstable at the time. My husband at the time did not want me to go through with the divorce. In an attempt to keep me from leaving, I was more or less tricked into becoming pregnant.

My doctor decided that I was not physically well enough to bring this child into the world. I decided to have an abortion.

I made the appointment to have the abortion and at the same time to have my fallopian tubes tied off – to prevent a further pregnancy. Both were hard, hard decisions.

In 1975, I began experiencing the overwhelming desire to have a child. I also knew deep inside that the earlier baby I couldn't carry was to have been a little girl. I don't know how I knew that it was a little girl. I just knew.

One day, I was at a beach. Sitting there watching the sun setting over the waves, I began to pray. I prayed to our Father, the Creator of us all, who can do anything. This is the way I have always thought of God. He can do anything. There is nothing that He cannot do. So this afternoon at the beach, I went to Him. Even though I felt unworthy and totally undeserving and actually had little hope of such . . . I asked God for my child back.

Later that night, I was just dozing off and was in that part of sleep where you are not really asleep, but you are also no longer awake . . . when I seemed to be visited by three men. They came and talked to me. They told me that I was going to be a mother and that it would be a little girl. The men told me that I would be getting my child back, yes, the one that I had given up so many years ago! Unbelievable!

At that time, I was dating the man who eventually became my husband. He was a therapist. I went to him and told him of the visit. He thought I was totally out of my mind. He knew that I had my tubes tied and could not have children. As a therapist, I guess he was used to dealing with this sort of thing. He took the whole story with a grain of salt. However he was curious and asked, "Nancy, who are these men that are coming to you?"

I replied, "I don't really know, but they are telling me that I am going to be a mother."

"Well, for gosh-sake, find out who/what they are! "

"Yes, good advice."

That night as I went to sleep, thank goodness – thank God, they came again. After that, they came every night for the next three weeks. They told me things that were going to happen. These were things which ultimately did in fact occur. Actually I might have found it difficult to experience them if the three men had not forewarned me and made me believe that they were angel-type beings.

During these visits, the three men told me to prepare
myself. On the last night, as a part of this preparation, they
seemed to take me to a special place. There was an angel
there who appeared to me in the form of man. I don't know
how I knew all of this, but the knowledge of what I was seeing
just came into my consciousness as a part of the experience.
This man was holding a child's hand. The child was a little girl,
about 18 months old, dark hair, dark eyes. She was a beautiful
little child. I was not allowed to talk to her, or make any advance
toward her. I was only allowed to observe her. I realized that
this was to let me see the child that I was going to be receiving.
That was the last experience of the last of the visits of the three
angel men.

In the years which followed, much of what I was told
in fact occurred. The man whom I had been dating and I were
married. We studied for the ministry and became ordained
ministers. Oddly, however, during this time, we performed only
one single wedding ceremony. In fact, my husband and I
performed it jointly.

The joint ceremony was for a couple who were expecting
a child. The woman was someone whom my husband and I had
known for some time. [In fact, I realized later that she had even
been in attendance at our ordination.]

The mother went on to have her baby, a little girl whom
she named Tonya. When the child was 18 months old, her
mother died. Circumstances were such that the little girl came
to live with us. Eventually we were privileged to legally adopt
her. It makes me so happy to be able to say that she has been and
is now our beloved daughter.

I believe she is the soul incarnate of the child I gave up. She was meant to be my child. I knew that my prayers were being answered. God gave me this child again.

So you see, Tonya was to be with us all through this, just as the angels said she would be. She was to be and is God's gift to us. That is what is so wonderful about this experience, how loving and forgiving our Father in Heaven is to us.

Today I know that God loves all of us so very much. The angels have been good to me many numbers of times; but this will always be the most special time.

Barbara's Story

An Angels' Chore

There was an incident which happened a couple of years ago which I thought was pretty unusual. It was in the dead of winter. It was a bad, bad day. My husband Charlie had to go out somewhere. He was on the freeway I guess and a tire "blew."

He pulled over and got out of the car. He was standing there looking at the tire. I guess he thought it was going to fix itself. Anyway, he was standing there looking at the tire and this man came up behind him. He was a young fellow in a truck. He got out and asked if he could help.

This was two o'clock in the afternoon. Charlie told him what had happened. They both agreed that there wasn't much left of the tire. Charlie had to ruin it getting off of the freeway.

This young fellow stayed with Charlie. He took him to a place that sold the kind of tires that Charlie liked. (He always liked to keep good tires on the car.) Anyway, this young man went and carried Charlie to buy a new tire – then brought him back and helped him put the tire on the car.

They went by the fellow's house and got something to eat and drink. In short, he fooled with Charlie all afternoon before he finally got him back on the road. Charlie called me and told me what had happened. You know, that he was all right and everything. He told me all about this fellow helping him. Anyway, it was almost dark before he made it back, but he got home in one piece.

The next morning, Charlie said, "I want to send that fellow some money. This guy took a lot of his time to help me. I think we ought to send him something."

I said, "Fine, what do you think that we ought to send him?"

We decided how much we thought we could afford. It certainly wasn't as much as his time was worth probably, but we wanted to send him something. I picked up the phone and called the number Charlie had insisted on getting. (I wanted to ask him for his address.) I identified myself when he answered and said, "You know, you're an angel."

He replied, "I've been called many things in this life, but angel was never one of them."

I said, "Well, I feel like you're an angel." And I did. I did feel like that.

He said, "You know, that was funny yesterday. I was off from work. I decided to go out to the lake and just mess around. The weather was too bad to fish. I just wanted to get out of the house for a while."

This fellow continued, "I passed by this car with a man standing by it looking down at the wheel. It was so cold, down in the low teens. It had just started sleeting. The weather was really bad that day."

He said, "I passed on by. But just as I did, it was as if a voice spoke up inside of me. Something told me to stop and help the old man. It said that he was going to die if I didn't go back there and help him."

This fellow told me he went down to the next corner and turned right. He circled the block and came up behind Charlie. Of course, Charlie didn't know all of that. He just knew that somebody came up behind him and stopped.

Anyway, he said it was odd how the voice, whatever, had just said to him, "If you don't stop and help him, that old man is going to die and it isn't quite time yet."

I think that he was a bit touched by the experience, too. Anyway, that was the last that I ever heard of the man. Whether he was an angel or not, I don't know. If he wasn't, he was sure doing an angel's work.

Note: Hundreds of "Charlie's" friends and his loving family were so grateful to have a couple more years with "Charlie." He had a talent for giving joy and uncondi-tional love to everyone who knew him. He went on to be with his God in Heaven when he was almost 90.

Helen's Story

Fourteen Angels

I was very ill with bronchitis. I had been in bed for several days. My temperature would not go down.

One night, I sat up in bed. I said, "I have done all that I know how to do. I've got to be released from this."

During the night, I could feel the bronchitis, the illness moving. I felt it settling into my left lung. Then, I began to feel this massaging of my left lung.

My body around the lung was being massaged. It was so noticeable that it startled me. It woke me up. I said, "What is this?"

There was a reply. It said, "We are your 14 angels. We have come to make you well."

So time went on. The first Sunday after all of this, I went to church. The minister said, "I have special music today. The soloist will now sing *Fourteen Angels*."

I had never heard of that song, before or since. It was so beautiful.

*Note: If it is true that our souls each have an assignment upon coming to earth – that is, a purpose which needs to be fulfilled; perhaps the friend who told me this experience was a bit behind schedule and simply needed to get on about the work of it and was given a boost.

Glenda's Story

Hill Country Vista

My dad grew up in the hill country of Texas. He was a hunter. He grew up being a hunter. His father died when the children were very young. Dad was the oldest child. During the years of the great depression, he hunted in order to feed the family. Those were hard years. Without his hunting skills, they might not have made it.

Throughout his life, he continued to hunt. His favorite thing to do was to go deer hunting. He and my mother often went hunting together. They had many loving experiences hunting together.

My dad died of cancer. We took his body back home to the hills he loved. We knew that he wanted to be laid to rest there. We carried out his wishes.

We buried him in his home town of Centerpoint, Texas. We picked a small cemetery, one out in the country. It sat up on top of a lovely vista. The cemetery looked out across a valley. At the back of the valley, there was a large open meadow, nestled in against a backdrop of foothills.

We held a memorial service at the grave site. Just as it started, a single shot rang out in the distance. It echoed off the surrounding hills, and rolled towards us from across the valley floor. When we looked up, there in the distance were three of the most beautiful deer you have ever seen. They ran single file right across the meadow. It was as though, in perfect fashion, they had crossed behind his casket.

Looking from where we were standing, there was the casket before us, with this beautiful line of deer crossing behind it as they headed up into the foothills.

Everyone there that day understood the message. Everybody who knew him felt like it was a perfect departure. We knew that my dad was going to his happy, hunting ground. It was really a very moving experience for us all.

Debra's Story

Angel of Passage

My experience happened the day before Valentine's Day.
I was out on the road on a business trip.

In a motel that night, I was saying my prayers. I was
telling God that I knew that the next day was Valentine's Day.
I was saying that for the first time, I hadn't hoped for, or wished,
or had anxiety over not having a boyfriend in my life. I knew
that I wasn't going to receive flowers or anything like that. As I
spoke, it just came out that God was going to be my valentine
that year. I realized that being close to Him was really what
mattered.

I fell asleep. It was raining the next morning when I
awoke. It was about eight o'clock. I was just slightly awake, laying
there, listening to it rain.

Suddenly, I felt someone tucking me in on my left side.
Of course, it was quite a shock! Then, in a split second, I
heard a flapping of wings above me. Whatever it was landed
on the right side of me. In that instant, I opened my eyes.

To the right of me was this tremendous bright, white light.
It was so overwhelming, so powerful, so bright. I just lay there,

frozen in amazement. As this was happening, I could feel it loving me. I could actually feel the angel's love for me.

Then, I heard something being said. I couldn't make it out. It was like the angel was trying to say something to me. After that, the light (that I somehow knew was an angel energy) became fainter and disappeared.

I realized that in actuality, God was sending a message to me in response to my prayer the night before. I really think that what God was saying was, "I love you. I am here for you."

He was comforting me and tucking me in. I can't explain it any better than that. It was like an angel of passage for me.

When I heard the wings and saw the bright white light, the loving, the beauty of it all, the immensity; I knew that it was an angel from God. It was confirmation of God's love for me, that we are here together. I am not alone. None of us are here alone.

Praise Singing

Angel presence-angel light
Guard us both-by day and night

You who hover by your flight
To maintain balance and your might

We are grateful for your gaze
And your love in His great ways

Thank you for these helpful ways
Always singing to God's praise

Along The Journey . . .

As my understanding has grown, of angels and their daily
presence in our lives, of God and His incredible love for us,
I have gotten more accustomed to looking for the work of God
and His angels in this world. Because of what I have learned,
and of what I have come to believe, hardly a day goes by that I do
not experience some contact with the secret world of the angels.
Some days their miracles appear in my own life, other days I can
see their work in events reported on the news. I have learned
to see the work of God's angels in my world.

In this way, my world has become a much gentler place.
This understanding has also changed the way that I look
at my life and the world around me. With the growth of my
faith, this world, this life has become more of something
to observe rather than judge. I especially love to observe nature
and quiet moments.

Secret Place

In this quiet place...

there is peace.

In this quiet place...

there is only the sight of God's natural beauty enjoying itself.

In this quiet place...

there is only the smell of living growth lifting towards the sun.

In this quiet place...

there is only the sound of water trickling down over the rocks.

In this quiet place...

there is only the touch of the wind angel's barely-there caresses.

In this quiet place...

there is only the taste of mother-earth's nourishments.

In this quiet place...

there is the peace of angel love.

Thank you, God

Jane's Story

An Angel Watching
Over Her

oming home from work one afternoon, I was just a few
feet from my driveway when a motorcycle officer zoomed
by. He had his lights flashing and his siren going.

As he sped past me, I looked up into our driveway.
I could see that my daughter's car wasn't there. At almost the
same instant, I very distinctly, very clearly heard a voice
from somewhere around my right shoulder. The voice said,
"It's Christy."

Christy is my daughter. I knew she was running around that
day. She was practicing for drill team and running errands.
I thought, "Well?" Almost instinctively, I decided to follow
the motorcycle. Although it wasn't in the direction I thought
Christy could have been going, I blindly followed anyway.

I met the ambulance coming back the other way. It had
no lights on, no lights flashing. I thought, "Something must to
be terribly wrong." I went on to see about the car.

Sure enough, just up ahead was her car. It was lying in a ditch upside down. She had "rolled" the car as she was going around a curve. She had obviously lost control of the car and the car had propelled itself over the curb and hit a concrete bridge abutment. The car had landed on its roof and then slid into the abutment on its passenger side. The impact squeezed the car almost in two. The car was just "buckled" like an accordion. My heart felt like a sledgehammer beating inside my chest. I had trouble getting my breath. Looking at the damage to the car it was hard to imagine anyone surviving the crash.

After I identified myself as Christy's mother, the police officer at the scene told me that they had already loaded her into the ambulance. He said they were just taking her to the hospital to be checked, but that, incredibly, she seemed to have survived the crash and be unhurt.

Later at the hospital when I asked her how she had managed to get out of the car, she said, "One of my friends pulled me out. Tom pulled me out."

We wanted to thank him for what he had done so we approached as he waited in the hospital hallway. He said he wasn't there and that he didn't do it! He was the first person to be at the scene of the wreck. He even remembers being the first one to help her. I remember seeing him there when I stopped to speak to the police. But he swears that when he got there, she was already out of the car.

To this day, Christy will say, "I know that he was there. He was just excited and doesn't remember." Tom says that he didn't come up until afterwards. He said that no one was around when he got there, but that Christy was laying outside of the car.

I believe the only way that Christy could have gotten out of that car was with angelic help. If you had seen what the car looked like, you would understand. It was completely totaled. She had to have received help in order to come through that kind of a wreck without being hurt. At the scene, we could all smell gasoline. With the car flipped over, it was dripping everywhere. You could smell it. I don't know why it didn't catch fire. There had to have been help from an angel who got her out of the wreckage.

I feel like it was an angel that told me to go to Christy. I think that another angel was sent to watch out for her and to get her out of the car. It was the only way that I can explain what happened.

The most wonderful thing about the entire experience is that I didn't feel any fear. The whole time, it was like I knew that she was being taken care of. I knew that the angel was keeping her safe.

Note: I believe Christy had a soul purpose yet to be fulfilled. God sent angel help in order for it to continue to be accomplished.

Nancy's Story

Rescuing Angel

The funeral for Dr. Martin Luther King was just over. The procession of mourners had left the Ebenezer Church and was coming down Auburn Street in Atlanta, Georgia. It was a day of turbulent emotion for people everywhere, who were shocked by the tragic event. Some, anguished by the assassination and overwrought with grief, were venting their anger and frustration through violent responses.

My sister, Nancy, was at the time a young, married, working mother. The office where she worked was located along the route of the funeral procession. Since radio and TV stations had been broadcasting warnings of possible riots, Nancy's boss released her from work early so she could pass through the troubled area ahead of the crowd. She had to pick up her 13-month old baby son at the nursery and pass through downtown Atlanta to go home.

She hurried to the nearby parking lot where she regularly left her car. It was owned and operated by a black family with whom she was well acquainted. The parking attendant, one of the family members, promptly brought her car to her. She got in and started on her way. Anxious about the possibility of a riot, she wanted to get out of the area as soon as possible.

When she tried to enter the street, however, the crowd converged on her car, blocking her path. Fearful that her car could be turned over, she looked for the parking attendant – but could only see the angry mob who had surrounded her car. She was terrified. An unwilling prisoner, trapped in her car, she feared for her life.

What happened next was hard to believe. Suddenly, the crowd fell back as a man cut through it to get to her. She saw that, although the man who spoke to her was a white man, he wore a blue shirt marked with the parking lot's logo. It was the same uniform as the one worn by the other parking attendant. When he tapped on the car window and spoke to her, she cracked the window to hear what he said.

"Turn on your headlights in honor of Dr. King, and go on down this street," he instructed her. "You will be fine. Just be sure to keep your headlights turned on and you'll get home safely."

While she did not recognize the man who spoke to her, she followed his instructions. When she turned on her headlights and drove into the street, the crowd parted so she could pass through it. Without incident, she drove to the nursery, picked up her son and, keeping her headlights turned on in honor of Dr. King as she had been instructed, traveled through the downtown streets and arrived home safely.

The next week, when she was back in her working routine, she wanted to thank the people at the parking lot for their help. When she parked her car at the lot, she gratefully told her familiar parking attendant, "I want to thank you and another one of your employees who was so kind to me the other day."

The attendant didn't seem to know who she was talking about.

"You know, the white fellow who was working here," she explained. "He told me to turn on my headlights."

"White man?" the attendant asked, puzzled. "There isn't any white man who works here."

"But he had on your uniform – the blue shirt with your logo."

He shook his head. "As you know, this is a family operated business, and none of us are white men. We don't have any white employees."

There was no denying the man's sincerity, but neither was there any question in my sister's mind about her experience with the parking attendant who had helped her. She remembered how the crowd had parted for him when he came to her aid, and she clearly remembered following his instructions. There could be no doubt about the event she had experienced, nor could there be any question that something very unusual had happened to her. The only explanation for the occurrence that she could find was that the man was an angel who had been sent to help her.

Lynda's Story

Parking Angel

A friend of mine named Lynda is somewhat famous for calling upon her guardian angel.

It seems that a few years ago she needed to purchase a gift for a Christmas party she was planning to attend. She needed to go to a certain store to get it.

The problem was that she had her two little boys with her. You know how little boys can be pretty wild when they are ages two and three. They were quite a handful. When she went shopping it seemed as if she had to pull and drag them around.

So on this day, she was trying to figure out how she was going to get her shopping done with the kiddos along. It was the holiday season and the stores were crowded. She was not looking forward to having to drag those two little boys through the parking lot and the store.

While talking to an older friend of hers, she mentioned her predicament. She told her friend, "If I could just find a parking place up near to the store, I wouldn't have to 'drag' those boys so far."

Her older friend looked at her and replied, "Well, I always ask my guardian angel to get me a parking place. When I ask, my angel tells me right where a good place is going to be."

Her friend continued, "Just go on to the store and when you get there, picture in your mind where the right place would be. Just see it. Where would the right place be?"

So my friend Lynda loaded up those two boys and went on to the store. As she was pulling into the shopping center, she said that she pictured up in her mind's eye a parking space right out in front of the store. Then she said, "Angel, could you find that for me? Could you do that for me, please?"

She didn't really believe that it was going to work, but she drove on into that part of the parking lot anyway. When she got closer to the front of the store, she could see a parking spot right where she had asked for it!

She could hardly believe her eyes. She was delighted. She made her purchase and was in and out of the store before the boys even thought about getting restless.

Lynda got into the habit of asking her angel to find her parking places. Now this has gotten to be such a common event with Lynda that her friends joke about it. They say, "Oh, let's let Lynda drive. She always gets a great parking spot."

A whimsical thing? Maybe so. Maybe angels have fun, too.

Fran's Story

Reaching For My Angel

 while back I was consumed with fear. I was completely out of touch with God. My mind was whirling and churning with "what ifs." I could not pull myself out of it. As time passed, it seemed to get worse.

My fears became terrors. I could not sleep. I could hardly function when awake. I went to my doctor for a severe pain in my arm and shoulder. He began the medical process of diagnosis and soon sent me to see a specialist. The specialist sent me out for tests and eventually to another doctor. This went on for several weeks.

One after the other, each doctor would say that they had discovered something that looked serious. Then, it would require another test, an x-ray, CAT SCAN or ultrasound would have to be run. Each time there was a waiting period of several days before I would hear the results.

This one particular night, while waiting to hear back from one of the doctors, I lay in bed in the dark. It was about four o'clock in the morning. I was exhausted but could not seem to quiet my mind enough to sleep.

In desperation, I began to pray. I do not think that I was even saying words really. I was reaching up to my Higher Power to rescue me. I felt as if I was at my wits end. I didn't know where to turn next.

My eyes were closed so I did not see the angel when he came to me, but I felt something surround me. I kept my eyes closed for fear that if I opened them this being which was giving me such a feeling of peace and comfort would leave. Gradually, my fears began to dissipate. My body began to relax. I felt protected. I felt loved.

It seemed as if a long time passed, but I am sure that it was just a few minutes. I spoke out loud, "Are you my guardian angel?" I seemed to get a reassuring response in return. Then I was able to simply drop off to sleep. I slept deeply and awoke refreshed the next morning. Before I had been awake very long, my fears tried to return. I closed my eyes, put out my hand and again felt my angel near me.

Since that time I have found it best to remember my angel daily, and when I do – I receive that same sense of assurance . . . loving spiritual assurance. I eventually recovered my health. Now when life throws up a road block, I just put out my hand and my angel is there for me.

Note: Fran, we are proud of you.

Ben's Story

Christmas Angel

I had an experience when I was about three years old which has stayed with me ever since. It was Christmas Eve night. I had been asleep but woke up and had to go to the bathroom. I climbed out of my bed. I heard a noise, so I looked out of the window. I saw my mother and father getting gifts out of the trunk of the car.

I went on toward the bathroom. As I passed the doorway to the living room I saw something out of the corner of my eye so I looked in that direction. Standing right there was Santa Claus. In the flesh, as a man, was the perfect Santa Claus. If you can imagine what Santa Claus would look like, that was him. He was standing by the Christmas tree. He was smiling. He looked jolly and happy. At first I thought it was my daddy dressed up – but I remembered just seeing my daddy outside.

When Santa saw me, he put his finger up to his lips and said, "Shhhhh . . ." He smiled again, and then looked back to the Christmas tree.

I took off running. It really scared me. That is all about the experience itself that I remember.

Afterwards, I told my parents about it. They didn't really believe my story so I didn't tell anyone else about it . . . ever . . . until now.

It was quite an experience for me though. It was as if one of God's angels had come with a message of promise for me. I knew "in the depths of me" that this was a God-gift to me. Since then, no matter what has happened I have felt loved and a bit "special." After all, not everyone has had a personal visit from Jolly St. Nick.

Note: We think it is good, Ben, that you do feel "special" –
     Yea, God, for giving you the experience.

Charles' Story

Gabriele

bout ten years ago, I was living in south Florida. My wife and I, and our young children were celebrating a very joyous Christmas Eve. I remember that things were really going well in our lives. We were all happy and healthy. It was a beautiful Christmas Eve to be sharing as a family, the kind that you would look back to years later, in remembrance.

We were just sitting down to dinner when there was a knock at the door. I opened it to find a very attractive young lady in her early twenties. I had never seen her before.

She quickly explained, "I am between planes on my way to the west coast. Someone at the airport told me that quite possibly you might welcome a stranger."

We told her that of course we would and asked her in. She immediately sat down to dinner with us.

She was apparently from some place in southern Europe. She spoke with a lovely accent. She told the most beautiful stories. We were fascinated by her accounts of all the places she had seen and the things she had done. She made us all feel very happy.

After about three hours, she got up to return to the airport. I walked her to the door. As she was leaving I said to her, "We didn't even ask your name."

She replied, "My name is Gabriele." With that, she stepped outside and closed the door.

I stood there for just an instant, a matter of only a few seconds. I thought to myself, "I need to get an address, a last name – I've got to know something more about how to get in touch with her."

I opened the door. She was gone. There was nothing. She had walked through the door and it was as though she had simply vanished.

Our family has considered the incident to have been a true angel experience – one bringing good tidings and cheer.

Lois' Story

The Greatest Gift

My mother had a very good friend. They were such good friends that they called each other "sister," even though they were no relation. This woman's brother was in the hospital. He was dying. The woman asked my mom to come up there and help her "be with him." My mom agreed and after her work she met her friend at the hospital. She sat on one side of the bed and her friend sat on the other. They just sat there, from time to time taking one of the man's hands to comfort him. My mom had worked all day. She was already very tired. But they sat like this, just holding onto his hands. Mom said that it was as if they were just there, waiting for him to pass on.

The hours went by and it started getting very late. My mom looked at her watch and it was almost midnight. She hated to do it, but decided that she would have to leave and go home.

She squeezed the man's hand and put it down on the bed. She was thinking, "I have a family. I have to get up and go to work in the morning. I just can't stay here all night."

She said that as she was thinking this, all of a sudden, the angel of death appeared over the head of the bed on the wall.

As she told me this story, she said, "So you will know, the angel of death is not this big, black hooded skeleton, carrying his scythe. It's really this gorgeous angel, as big as a whole wall. It's like 20 feet high and 20 feet across, with huge golden wings. It's really beautiful."

Anyway, she said that this gorgeous, golden angel appeared over her friend's brother's bed. She said that the angel spoke to her and said, "Just five more minutes. Just wait five more minutes."

So, my mom said that she took up the man's hand again and held it. She said that she sat there, looking at her watch to note the time. Sure enough, it was exactly five minutes later that the man suddenly opened his eyes. Quickly, she leaned down and whispered in the man's ear, "Look for the light." She did not know the man's religious or spiritual background, so she just held his hand and told him to look for the light.

She whispered, "When you see the light, go to it. Just follow the light. There is nothing to fear."

My mom said that with those words, the man took a breath and was gone.

It was years ago that this all happened and that Mom first told me the story. I remember thinking when she told me, "That is so wonderful. I wish I could see angels." That was the way it was for my mom. She could see things that other people just could not see. I never have seen angels like she apparently could. She would tell me about them, but I just could never see like she could. Apparently, she had been this way all of her life. It was the only way that she had ever known to be. It was just a part of who she was. It was not as if

I didn't believe in angels. It is just that I couldn't see them as she apparently did.

About a month before my mom died, we became extremely close. We had always been close, but you know how it is with someone who is dying. You spend a lot of time together. You can talk about things more freely, especially the subject of death. During this time, I spent a great deal of time just sitting and talking with her. You think that you have been close to someone for twenty years, but when you know that the end is near, you really want to spend all of the time with them that you can.

My mom had known that she had terminal cancer for about a year. Many people came to see her during this period. She had many friends who loved her. They would tell her that she did not have to accept it, her terminal condition. They said that she could fight it, that she didn't have to let the cancer kill her. They told her many things in their attempts to comfort both her – and I suspect – themselves. Now you have to understand that normally, my mother would not sit and listen to anyone try to convince her about his or her version of spiritual truth. She knew what she believed and that was good enough for her. She had her own understanding, based upon what she could see. She would never try to force her views on another person. In the same way, she didn't feel that you had the right to force your views on her. So, normally, if someone was to try to tell her how she should be thinking, she would stop them right in the middle, thank them for what they were trying to do, but otherwise [perhaps in a symbolic way] walk away before even letting them finish.

However she wasn't doing these kinds of things with her visitors now, so one day I said, "Since you became terminal, you allow all kinds of people from all kinds of religions to come and do their spiel. You don't stop them."

She just smiled and replied, "Well, this is their way, in their own heart, of doing what is best to help me. So I allow them their say. I'm doing it more for them than for me anyway."

She and I were closer than ever that month before she died. One day, we were just sitting there talking and tears started streaming down her face. I remember that I thought to myself that she must be seeing something, another of her visions.

After a few moment she said, "There is the most gorgeous angel standing right here in front of us."

As always, I couldn't see a thing. Mom continued, "It looks like the angel of death. It's huge, very tall. Its wing span covers the entire room. Its golden, beautiful."

I thought, "Oh my God, it's here for her."

As if she knew what I was thinking, Mom said, "It's just letting me know not to be afraid when the time comes. But don't worry. Everything will be fine when my time comes. You will be fine. It will be easy and natural."

We took Mom to the hospital one last time. They said there was nothing more they could do but send her home with some strong pain reliever medication. I remember that I tried asking the doctor how long she would have. He told me that he was not God and really could not know.

He went on to say that the best person to ask was probably my mom. On the way home, I remember thinking, "There is no way that I can ask my own mother how much time that she has got. I just won't do it."

We got her home and I stayed there with her. She was bedridden. When the hospice people came out to check on her that evening, I told them that I would be surprised if she were to make it through the weekend.

The next night, Thursday, she had some bad pain. I gave her some medication but it did not seem to help. It was extremely upsetting to see her in the pain and I called Hospice to ask for suggestions to make her more comfortable. I didn't know what to do. Her pain medication had always been strong enough to work. They told me what to do. We ended up giving her a tremendous amount of pain medication, which just knocked her out. At last she was sleeping peacefully and seemingly free of pain. She slept all Thursday night and all day Friday.

Then on Saturday morning, while I was sitting on the bed beside her holding her hand – she just took in a breath and let it out – and she was gone. It was exactly as she had always told me that it would be. She just quietly passed on.

All my life, my biggest fear had always been the knowing that someday my mother was going to die, and that when she did, I would just fall apart. Well, it wasn't like that at all. It was exactly like she said. It was the most beautiful thing. Her transition was the most wonderful thing. I remember thinking, "Okay, Mother, you win. You made a believer out of me."

When she passed, I watched her spirit literally go out from her head. Tears started streaming down my face. I know everybody in the family thought that I was crying because in their eyes she was dying. But I was crying for the wonder of what I had just watched. I had never seen anything like it in all of my life. I never saw things the way that she did. It was not that I didn't believe. I just had never been able to see the things that she could always see.

It is hard to describe what I saw in the moment that she passed. It was like the blending and swirling of water-color paints all running in together, or like smoke drifting up towards the sky. It was beautiful. Tears of joy were just streaming down my face. I was sitting there saying over and over, "You were right. You have been telling me this all of my life, but now I really know."

Everybody in the family was hovering over her. But she had told me that at that point not to hover, because she would no longer even be there. Everybody was doing just what she had said that they would do. They were all around the bed, and they were crying. I was crying too, but not for the same reason. And I wasn't looking down, I was looking up, because I knew that she was not down there in that body anymore. She was free.

I remember that I looked down at her one last time. I said to her, "Yes, you were right Mom, as usual. It was just the most beautiful thing, the greatest gift that a mother could give to her daughter. Thank you for arranging that with your angels so I could see it. Thank you. I love you. Thank you."

Bonnie's Story

Angel In The Clouds

 ary was my son. He passed away in June of 1977. He has been a part of so many spiritual experiences for me. There is one especially that I recall.

It was in the first October after his passing. My husband and I were on a flight to Miami. It was overcast. When we got up above the clouds, we could see rolling beautiful thunderhead clouds beneath us. It was something to see.

As I looked out at them, I thought to myself that it looked just like a lot of snow. With the sun reflecting off of them it reminded me of how we used to play with the kids out in the snow. We had always done that up north. As I was sitting there, I thought, "Gary would love this. Gary, I am sure that you are out there someplace."

All of a sudden, as I was sitting there looking out at the clouds and having this mental conversation with myself, I clearly felt Gary kiss me. I could actually feel his kiss, the lips upon my cheek.

I looked around at my husband. He was talking to another passenger and not even looking my way. In fact, he was sitting on the aisle, with a seat in between us.

I just knew that Gary had kissed me. It was like he was saying, "I am here Mom." It was such a beautiful experience. I have taken him with me ever since.

Note: What does this story have to do with angels? Maybe the angels were only acting as vehicles of passage in the clouds to help son – Gary, make a connection? My friend certainly felt as if son – Gary's extended life in that different dimension of consciousness brought a message of hope and peace – which is one function of angels.

Dorothy's Story

Angel of Peace

y very favorite picture of my mother and father is involved with an experience which I once had. It was a very healing experience for me. It was about forgiveness.

This picture portrays my mother and father as I want to remember them. It was taken well before their last days of frailty and ill health. They both died at the age of 94. This picture captures them in their healthier, younger days.

For many years, I had experienced a problem with forgiveness where my parents were concerned. This was especially true as it related to my mother. One day, as a part of a meditation, I found myself seeing this photograph in my mind.

There was a pink cloud that appeared in the sky of this picture. It was not a cloud with a great deal of volume. It was a long, flat sort of cloud, as if it were coming forth from deep within the picture.

As I watched, my mother and father left the picture frame and began receding into the cloud. They simply disappeared into this beautiful pink cloud.

About the same time they disappeared into the cloud, at the very front of the picture frame there appeared a very small angel. She had short wings and a tiny halo. The angel was flapping its wings for all it was worth. It was heading for the pink cloud.

As I looked closer, I realized that the angel's face was mine. It was as though I was the angel. As I flew into that cloud to join my parents, the heavens surrounding that cloud burst forth with life. Sun rays shot out in all directions. The cloud billowed and flashed with light.

A voice of great depth and power, a deep and resonate voice, spoke forth from the cloud. It said, "These are my beloved children in whom I am well pleased." I knew then that God has no grandchildren. We are all children of God filled with His peace and surrounded by His love [when we allow it]. I felt a new and sweet love for my parents as fellow travelers on this spiritual journey we call life. All my memories seem sweetened by the angel of peace that was sent to me that morning. Even though that was an experience seemingly only in my mind – it has had far-reaching results. Thank you, God.

Dale's Story

A Child Announced by Angels

My Laura is 37 years old and had undergone surgery to prepare for pregnancy. There were months of recuperation. Then, at last, the "go ahead" signal came from her doctor. There were weeks of prayer and concern about her tumors growing back – and more prayer. I read my *A Course In Miracles* devotional every day, trying to turn everything, with joy and gratitude, over to Him. Trying to know that all was well. But at night I would say "but heal my aching heart."

It was early morning, between waking and sleeping. It was not a dream! It was an insertion into my consciousness. They were grouped around me like girlfriends on a playground. Yet they sparkled, they were smiling, shining. I don't know if you would call them "angels" or good friends from another room or place. It was like girlfriends letting me in on a secret. "She's going to conceive in April." Then I glowed, "Really?!" Then they nodded and sparkled some more. I remember the silence, the stillness as if time and space stood still. It wasn't a dream. Yes, an intercession into time, space into my consciousness.

I came fully awake praying, "Oh God, can it be true?" Laughingly, I told Laura on the phone that day about my "dream."

Laura's periods have always been irregular so there were weeks of uncertainty. She began buying ovulation kits that were confusing and "pregnancy" kits that didn't work.

Laura works in a hospital. One day she felt so ill a nurse/friend took a blood sample. Later she came back from the lab saying, "You couldn't be more pregnant!" I was thrilled and thankful. I thought, "Oh well, April is long gone." I went with her for a sonogram where they pronounced her six weeks. A quick count on my fingers, while we were in the doctor's reception office, I practically shouted, "Laura, it was April! The angels were right!."

We have said ever since, that this child was literally "announced" by angels. Our baby's nursery is decorated with angels. Along with prayers from my dear friends and earthly "angels" she will grace this earth on January 19th. Do I believe in angels? No wings or harps of course, but eternal friends, messengers from God, angel thoughts and angel guardians. Yes, like little Natalie Wood in *Miracle on 34th Street*, "I believe, I believe, I believe."

Sherrie's Story

The Pink Shawl

She started off by telling me that before her experience with the angel she hadn't known or heard much about them. If the topic ever did cross her mind, she said she thought about them in past tense, as in times long ago. She had been abused as a child. Trauma that went on for years. As a result, she said she became skeptical and non-trusting of almost everyone and everything.

She eventually married, but because of the past trust issues, there was much doubt. She had a low sense of self. Although her husband tried to show her he loved her and "was there" for her, she knew they would eventually be divorced if she wasn't able to get a handle on her personal issues. She was at a low ebb in her life.

She had terrible nightmares and was almost to a point of being afraid to go to sleep. About 1 o'clock one morning she woke up from one of the worst nightmares she had ever had. There were demon-type creatures coming for her. She couldn't get away, there was no hope. She was terribly frightened. Yet she didn't want to wake her husband. She just lay there in a miserable lump under the bedclothes. After awhile she found herself praying, "Oh God, life has just got to be better than this. Please

take away these nightmares, take this fear away.
I am so tired of being afraid. Please, make me strong." She prayed
like that, crying and in great sincerity for a while, then there
seemed to come a soft glow on the ceiling. The glow became
more of a soft pink light, then it came into focus and became
a beautiful pink angel. As the angel came closer, she could see that
the angel was really all in white, but that she was wearing a pink
wrap or shawl of some kind. As she watched, the angel took off
her pink wrap and gently and with great love wrapped her in it.
The angel didn't speak, but ministered to her with such immense
love in her eyes and ways. She said to me, "All I could feel was
this immense, total love. I started knowing at that moment that
my life would be different. I knew I "counted" with God. My
tears of fright and sadness turned to tears of joy for being so greatly
loved." I almost couldn't believe that it had happened.

Her husband does not doubt that something happened.
He says that from that night, she started to change and is now a
much more secure and happy person. He believes in her angel.

Today she says of her childhood trauma and the
unhappiness of her life before her "angel experience" that, "It's
over. I'm stronger for it. I've been lifted in my discernment
of life. It was a miracle that changed my life. Everyday I thank
God all over again. I want to tell everyone that there really are
angels and God's love comes through them. I know I am a better
more loving person than before."

Brenda's Daughter's Friend's Story

An Angel to Show the Way

This happened to a friend of my daughter's before we moved to our present neighborhood. I'll call her Cheryl. Cheryl was riding her bicycle around the neighborhood when someone enticed, coerced or forced her into his car and abducted her. She had been with another young girl about her age (9) who went and told her mother what she had just witnessed. The police were called in right away. They told the distraught parents, however, that unless she was found in about four hours they would be looking for a body. Here was every parent's nightmare staring them in the face. Close friends of the family started a prayer chain and a young couple immediately came to their house and knelt at the living room couch in prayer.

Meanwhile, Cheryl was riding around in the car with her abductor. As she told it later, they had driven around for hours. Then, as he stopped at a particular corner, a man appeared at her window (which for some reason was open), reached his arm in and touched her arm. He said, "Get out of the car now." She and her abductor both turned to look at the man who had laid his hand on Cheryl's arm through the window. Cheryl said the man had spirals of light swirling around his head and it was all shining around his whole being. His voice and being held so much authority, she did as he said. Her abductor did not try to stop her. After she was safely out of the car, he sped away.

When Cheryl turned from watching the car drive off, the man who had spoken with her was nowhere to be seen. She began to walk down the street. She was drawn to a house down the middle of the block that was all lit up. Cheryl said the house was all lit up like a big sun behind it and all the rays were shooting out of the top and sides of the house. She walked up to the front door and rang the doorbell. It was opened by a man who happened to be a minister. He called her parents who were very happy to come and get her.

The minister told Cheryl's parents that he had been out all evening and had just come home through the back door. He said that he had no lights on in the house except his back den where he had just turned on the television and had heard about Cheryl's abduction over the news. He only turned on his porch light as he opened the front door to find her on his doorstep.

Also, as it turned out, he was the very minister that had officiated at the couple's wedding who had stayed and prayed with the family for Cheryl's safe return. The family believes that those prayers and others like them were what called in an angel and probably saved Cheryl's life.

Note: Again, most likely, Cheryl had not yet accomplished her earth assignment – her purpose. Life is a mystery, but that reason could make sense. For whatever reason, we are all most grateful her life was spared.

Elaine's Story

Teaming Up With Prayer

It was when my granddaughter was being born. I was in the birthing room with them. I wasn't planning to stay during the actual birth, but my daughter wanted me there so I was helping as best I could. It had been 2 1/2 hours of activity of the baby's head almost coming through, then going back into the birth canal. I knew my daughter was getting very tired and I was anxious as to why the actual birth was taking so long. You could see the bruise on top of the baby's head and the cone shape that was developing. I sensed that it was becoming a complicated delivery and I wondered where the doctor was.

Something caught my eye hovering just above my daughter. It was an angel of death. I became quite alarmed and started praying. I prayed, "Please take me up to the level where I can see what is happening and if it can be altered." I was shown (in my mind's eye) that the cord was wrapped around the baby's neck. About that time, with my daughter's next contraction, we could see that the skin of the head seemed to be turning blue. I began to pray in earnest for the highest good for all. For God to send light and life. For the doctor to come on! For the staff. For my daughter. For the baby. I prayed every way I knew how to pray! Just then the birthing room door flew open and the doctor rushed in. He had just delivered four other babies in consecutive order (so that's where he was). He immediately said, "My God, how long has this been going on?" And even while he was speaking, he did an episiotomy. The baby came out with the next contraction with the cord wrapped tightly around her neck and looking almost pale blue. She regained color shortly and began to cry lustily. We all breathed a sigh of relief. And I noticed that the angel of death was no longer there either.

My granddaughter is four now and is fine. She has developed quite normally. The only thing you might say is unusual about her is that she can also visually see angels like I do. I want to tell you her birth was one time I was really glad I have been privileged in this way.

Note: And we are glad for you and yours as well, Elaine. Another of God's miracles is revealed. Elaine is one of those unusual people who sometimes has what some people call "second sight." As she inferred, she has seen angels since childhood.

Angels Working In Unity

erhaps there is a way that I can best show the results of what I have learned thus far on my journey. Clearly there is one event, of which I was a part, which shows the power of God and His angels working in our lives.

One morning, around 6 a.m. the phone rang. When I answered, it was my father-in-law ("Dad") to us. He was calling from his apartment in his Retirement Village home.

"Billye," he said, "I need to speak to Jerry."

I passed the phone over to my husband. What had evidently happened was that Dad had been awakened by pain in his chest area during the night. It had already been several hours, and the pain was not subsiding. He had waited as long as he could before calling us.

Jerry told him to pull the emergency cord by his bed and to tell the attendants that he was on his way over. Jerry knew that it would be up to him to get Dad to the hospital. Dad wouldn't hear of going in an ambulance.

I met them at the hospital. They whisked Dad off to be checked by the chief resident on duty. We notified Dad's physician. He also soon appeared. During all of the watching, waiting and consultations, as to what had actually happened with Dad's heart, I was told "to go on home, do a few things, and come back later." It was just too early in the game to really know what had happened.

I had only been home about five minutes when I heard our dogs barking telling me someone was out front. To my surprise it was our daughter Karen who was supposed to be about three hours drive away at college. I asked, "Karen, honey, what are you doing home? You will miss your classes today. And I thought you also mentioned tests today and Monday??"

She explained that she had awakened suddenly around 3 a.m., and just <u>knew</u> that she was to come home. She said she couldn't go back to sleep because she kept thinking about her grandfather and felt as if she was being told to come home to Dallas. Finally – even though she had tests Friday and Monday and therefore had not planned to be coming home, she got up, dressed, left a note for her roommates and drove the miles home. "What's up? Did my angels want me here for Daddy's birthday tomorrow after all?" (My husband's birthday was the next day to add to it all). "Why did I need to come home? I know I am supposed to be here." I hugged her hard and told her that I didn't know either, but I was glad she was with us.

I told her what little I knew and we both went back to the hospital. Needless to say (since she was an excellent student and she could make up the tests once her instructors knew the circumstances), both her father and grandfather were also delighted with her surprise appearance.

Our son Michael, who was in medical school, had a rotation at the hospital where Dad had been taken. He could be with his grandfather some as well. While they used to live a distance away, after Mom's death, Dad moved to Dallas. Mike had spent many summers on their farm and he was particularly close to his grandad. That rotation time of a few weeks was the only time in his years in medical school that he was assigned to that particular hospital. That looks like another "Angel touch of God's love," doesn't it?

By the next day, Dad's doctors determined that the sac around his heart had "torn." To try to repair it would mean surgery that would be long and hard on him and might have poor (or worse) results anyway. We all prayed for guidance. I seemed to hear, "Trust in the Lord with all your heart and lean not unto your own understanding." It was a dark night of the soul time.

As with the last days of Mother Jones' passing, our strength came from a higher source. Our God also showed the Christ compassion (an early Church School teacher always said the scripture verse "Jesus wept" – while being the shortest verse in the New Testament – also described Jesus' great compassion for his friends). Our friends passed along the word of our family crisis. God's love moved through people that weekend in ways as tender as any mother's touch on a child's fevered brow.

Dad elected not to undergo the surgery. As he was alert and himself, his wishes were adhered to. He lived a few more hours and then died a peaceful death with his family around his bed holding his hands. We prayed a prayer of thanksgiving for his life and let him go on. He died on his only son's birthday telling us the great lesson of his life was that relationships were what life is all about. That love is the only real thing – only the loving is real. It was a sad time. It was a beautiful time. It was a holy time.

At every turn we could see the angels' loving touches to smooth the way. "God bless God" for the whole experience.

Especially for the children – his only grandchildren – being able to share it in close proximity. Those were two definite "God-touches."

Along the Journey . . .

If the telling of these happenings of *Angel Power, Angel Love* has helped someone to hold on – hold out – hold fast . . . to his/her faith in a loving God . . . my angel is smiling.

Epilogue

Today I thank God for what He has taught me along this journey. Today I know that I do not travel alone. Where I go, I go with the love of God, with the strength of my family, and the encouragement of those other spiritual travelers whom I meet along the way. Most of all, I know that I go with my dear angels – those chosen and assigned to me by my loving, heavenly parent. God and his miracles, angels and their wondrous powers will continue to be something of a mystery.

Along this journey I have been privileged to meet many wonderful, gifted people. As a result of their openness and honesty, I have learned a great many things. I know today that there is a God who loves me, who cares for me. I know that He loves me enough to have dispatched His angels to watch over me, to protect and to guide me and mine. What I know for me – is somehow even easier to know for you – for after all these inspiring stories you, too, must now realize that God is love – and that love is always a healing power. Love and only love is the ultimate reality.

Quote from my journal:

Beloved Billye (I love it when they do that . . . call me "beloved") . . . You people (humans) have been co-dependent on God's love and light every day. You, as a human family, are becoming more and more aware of this fact. Light is on a vibration of understanding, recognition and realization. The more it is seen for what it is . . . that is, looked at with the eyes of your awareness, it can come through any blocks you put up. These blocks come from your ignorance. They are merely immaturity of focus coming from your previous levels of unaware consciousness. Just have the intention to become more aware. And forgive yourselves. Forgiveness opens more blocks than any other single thing. Have the intention to focus on recognition of unseen help. It is there all around you. And one more thing . . . moment by moment, cherish and enjoy the precious moments of this 24-hours . . . this day. You are loved.

~ Us

Spirit Power

God's eternal flame
Always glowing bright
We are transformed
By your purple light

Bright in the night
In the midst of a storming
We do trust your love
With our souls' longings

And in the peace
Of an abiding heart
We thank you for your love
From our souls' deepest parts

How To Grow Closer To Your Angels

1. Have a quiet time each day when you center your mind God-ward . . . as in "Peace, Be Still."

2. Be willing to grow along spiritual lines — without outlining where that may lead you.

3. Consciously offer yourself, your service, your work to God's divine plan of love.

4. Ask your angels to be with you and to help carry out the plan of God's love through you.

Five Tips for Everyday Spirituality

1. *Wake up with "Good morning, God" as a first thought.* "This is the day the Lord has made, I will rejoice and be glad in it." Put yourself in his hands right away.

2. *Breathe.* Breathe in God, let go fear. Breathe in faith. Let go fear. Go outside and breathe in fresh air. Look at the trees. Try to find a bird to hear its song to the morning.

3. With a first cup of coffee, *read a devotional book/booklet* to reinforce that you and God are co-creators of your reality this day.

4. *Take a walk.* Use your large muscles to let the truth sink in that you are a spiritual being living in a physical universe. Look around you at your world in awareness, (i.e., a morning walk with God). Sing simple songs of praise and thanksgiving as you "walk with God."

5. *Journal with your Higher Power.* One easy way is to write a letter to your guardian angel and then at some point pretend that your angel writes you a note in response.

Do you have an angel story you would like to share?

Angels have touched many of us. If you would like to share your angel story with others please send it to:

Angel Power Productions
P.O. Box 12213
Dallas, Texas 75225

We are planning on offering more experiences telling of God's love.